HOW TO HIRE
THE PERFECT
EMPLOYER

HOW TO HIRE
THE PERFECT
EMPLOYER

Finding the Job and Career That Fit You
Through a Powerful Personal Infomercial

JIM BEQAJ

Foreword by Richard Nesbitt
Afterword by Tom Milroy

Toronto and New York

Published in 2011 by
BPS Books
Toronto and New York
www.bpsbooks.com
A division of Bastian Publishing Services Ltd.

ISBN 978-1-926645-36-0

Cataloguing-in-Publication Data available from Library and Archives Canada.

Cover: Gnibel
Text design and typesetting: Casey Hooper Design

Fit Factor, Personal Balance Sheet, Target Rich Environment, TRE, and Personal Infomercial are trademarks of Beqaj International Inc.

A portion of proceeds on sales of this book will be donated to The Sick Kids Foundation, Toronto.

To my wife,
Jennifer,
who has been so wonderfully supportive
and encouraging through all the ups and
downs of this difficult journey,
and my children,
Emma, Eddie, Nora,
Jack, Sam, and Sarah,
who inspire me every day

CONTENTS

Foreword ix

Preface xiii

Introduction 1

1   A Rude Awakening 7

2   What Do You Enjoy Doing Most? 19

3   Who Do You Work Best With, and Why? 43

4   What's Your Preferred Method for Resolving Conflicts? 61

5   How to Find Your Target Rich Environment 75

6   How to Present Your Personal Infomercial 93

7   How to Use Your Infomercial for Lasting Success 113

Conclusion 137

Afterword 139

FOREWORD

By Richard Nesbitt

When I returned from graduate school to Canada in 1986, I wanted to work for the best investment bank in the business, Wood Gundy. I tried the conventional approach through an investment banking associate position. No luck—that is, until a friend brought me in to meet the head of fixed income for Wood Gundy, Jim Beqaj. After fifteen minutes, Jim said, "I can work with this guy," and that was my life for the next ten years at Wood Gundy. It was the beginning of a trusted advisor relationship that has continued to this day.

Jim was my advisor and mentor from the time I helped set up a mortgage-backed security desk for him at Wood Gundy in 1986, again when I worked for him in New York in the mid-nineties, and then back in Toronto. His unique insights into people and business have been of great value to me in my more recent responsibilities as head of the Toronto Stock Exchange and now at CIBC.

Jim and I didn't operate the same way when we worked together. In fact, we solved problems and created programs in different ways. Jim was always able to conceive the big idea and attract people to the mission. I, meanwhile, liked to tease the best idea out of dozens of good ideas and bring focused resources to the task. Our approaches complemented each other as we worked through the years on many achievements.

Like Jim, I believe a business rises not on the technical skills of its employees but on how well those employees fit the culture of their business. Contrary to what you read in the business section of your daily newspaper, businesses that fail do not fail because of external factors but because of wrong decisions made by the people inside them. And these decisions, more often than not, emanate from problems of fit.

Let me put this more positively: Businesses succeed, and sustain their success, when their leadership teams are rowing in the same direction, and when their chief concern is to find and develop people who fit the culture of their business.

This book examines this critically important issue of fit from the point of view of individuals who are looking for the perfect employer. Leaders will also benefit greatly from this book, however, as they infer, from Jim's clear and compelling words, how important it is for them to refine their search for the perfect employees.

Richard Nesbitt is Chairman and Chief Executive Officer of CIBC World Markets Inc.

PREFACE

For so long (I'm talking decades, not years), I felt out of kilter in my work. Not only did I not fit my work, I didn't think it was even *possible* to fit.

I had some successful and exciting days in corporate life, but I also spent time on the outside looking in. I went through the painful process of taking responsibility for my life and figuring out why I didn't fit and how and where I could fit. I'm thrilled to say that the experience was far more liberating than it was painful. I emerged from this dark period to create a business that makes me so happy each and every moment of every single day, week in and week out, month after month, and year after year. If only I had discovered this earlier!

I've written this book because I've seen the process I developed out of my experience make such a genuine difference in the lives of the many people I have coached. It doesn't matter whether they're inside or outside the finance industry, already in a job or looking for one, new to the workforce or toiling at the most rarefied of senior levels—it works. While I don't believe anything is unique, I do know my process is helping people take responsibility for themselves—for everything in their lives from day one to this moment right now—and for how the world sees them.

I haven't written this book with the expectation of being the next Tom Peters or some other famous business writer but just to hold out hope to people caught in the very sad reality of work life today, the reality that only the tiniest percentage of people are actually doing what they truly love to do. My overall message for everyone reading this book is: *You can find your fit and love what you do.*

This book has been on my mind for a long time and I am thrilled that it is safely in your hands. Not being a prolific writer, I was fortunate to have the support and companionship of several people on my writing journey. Starting me off were writers David Thomas and David Hughes. Getting me over the goal line were my trusted advisor Lee Fullerton and my editor and publisher Donald G. Bastian. Cheering me on at every twist and turn were two very special friends, my business partners Jaz Chahil and Bob Baldock.

Of course none of this would have been possible without my wife, Jennifer. Thank you for your support and candidness when all seemed pretty bleak in the darkness of trying to find myself. I would have never made it and life would not be nearly as satisfying without you by my side, step by step, building to this day. And my thanks to Emma, Eddie, Nora, Jack, Sam, and Sarah–my six wonderful children, who teach me something new every day (and submit to being my guinea pigs as I develop my theories about people).

I will be forever indebted to Tom Milroy, for giving me my first assignment and believing in me when I was at my lowest point. Thank you, Tom. And thank you, Richard Nesbitt, for your friendship and support through the years.

As for my clients who have supported me from the very beginning—I am deeply grateful for your loyalty and trust and for inviting me into the inner workings of your business. What an honor!

Jim Beqaj

INTRODUCTION

I couldn't help but smile when I read a cover story in *The Economist* on the state of business today. Do you know what it identified as the number-one challenge of organizations big and small?

Finding the right people.

I smiled because I work as a trusted advisor to numerous clients, helping them with their recruiting, consulting for them on business matters, and coaching them. I coach many individuals who are looking for a job or considering a career change, or who wish to develop greater clarity and success in their present position.

Do you know what most of the people I work with say is *their* number-one challenge?

Finding the right employer.

I often wonder why companies can't find the right people. And why people can't find the right companies.

It would take a much thicker book than this to go into all of the causes of this colossal mismatch. However, I have developed an approach that is doing its part to successfully bring these two sides together. I call it the Fit Factor™, and in this book I want to use this approach to give *you* a whole new take on finding and developing a job and career. My approach will move you from hoping to be picked by an employer from among hundreds of applicants to being in the driver's seat. From being just another person queuing up for another pro forma interview to actually interviewing employers to see if they are the right fit for you.

As a result of reading this book, you will:

- Stop waiting beside your mailbox for that unlikely acceptance letter in response to passively sending out a résumé
- Find the employer *you* want to "hire" because it both needs you and wants you and is a place where you know you can add value

I want to help you determine:

- What you enjoy doing most (this will reveal what you're good at)
- Who you work best with, and why (this will reveal your wiring, or personality type)
- Your preferred method of resolving conflicts
- Your Target Rich Environment™ (TRE™)—the types of employers who fit you and your goals—companies where you should therefore concentrate your search

Armed with this personal information, you can then script and present a powerful Personal Infomercial™.

You know what an infomercial is. You're surfing the channels on your TV and pause when you hear something like:

You want to keep warm when you're feeling chilled, but you don't want to raise your heating bill. Blankets are OK, but they can slip and slide, and when you need to reach for something your hands are trapped inside. Now there's the Snuggy, the blanket that has sleeves.

What happens? If the opening words are true of you, you most likely will be drawn into the infomercial and you may even reach for your credit card after the pitch. If the words are not true of you, you will resume your surfing. (By the way, there is another answer to the problem posed by the infomercial above: an innovative product called *clothes*.)

In the same way, you're going to pitch your infomercial to employers who *need* what you have to offer. More than that, you will learn how to use your infomercial to find out whether the companies that *need* you also *want* you—you with your personality, your preferred style of working, and your goals. You will tell them in a few choice sentences what you're good at, who you work best with, and how you can add value.

You may feel a bit squeamish about the word "infomercial," but like it or not, you have one now. We all do. If you ask people how they see you, their response will reflect your current infomercial.

In fact, there are probably many different, muddled versions out there. What you need is one clear, consistent version. One that arms the interviewer with the words they need for describing you to the one who makes the hiring decision.

The point of having a powerful Personal Infomercial is simply this: Either you design how the world sees you or you let the world see you how it wishes.

Once you're in your new position, you will continue to use your infomercial. It will become second nature to you. It will be part of every conversation you have when the topic is you. Your infomercial is the key not only to getting a job but also to enhancing that job. You will use it to empower you as you move along to greater and greater fit in your career.

If developing and using a Personal Infomercial is the main point and value of this book, its core belief is this: *Each of us is responsible for our own life. We must take ownership of everything that has led us to where we are right now, today.*

The truth is, if you are going to find your best fit, you must take responsibility, going forward, for knowing yourself, defining yourself, and creating a clear and accurate perception of you.

I learned the importance of taking responsibility for myself and finding the right fit the hard way. The dramatic rise and fall I experienced in the first twenty-five years of my career forced me to take my life apart and put it back together again. This book is the result of what I learned. I believe the process I forged out of my experience will prove to be of great value to you.

A Rude Awakening

THERE IS ONLY ONE SUCCESS—
TO BE ABLE TO SPEND YOUR LIFE IN YOUR OWN WAY.

Christopher Morley

IF SOMEONE HAD ASKED ME DURING MY TWENTY-FIVE-year career in finance whether I loved doing what I did—whether I fit my job—I wouldn't have known what to say. I wouldn't have even thought of asking the question.

I was known for consistently building businesses and producing big numbers. My bosses kept giving me greater and greater responsibilities.

"What does fit have to do with it?" I would have asked.

In this chapter I want to show you how my ignorance on this point set me up for a very big fall. I believe my story will:

- Highlight how important it is for you to take responsibility for your career
- Help you redefine the concept of job and career fit

- Set you up for the transformational journey you'll be
  taking with me in this book

Getting Started

I come from hard-working immigrant parents. My father
died when I was ten, and one year later I started helping out
in our family restaurant in Ottawa, Ontario, where it was
all work, all the time—weekends, Christmas, March break,
summers.

We spoke Albanian at home. As an immigrant family, we
were not well integrated into society. As a kid I often felt out of
place. I grew up living with my mother in a duplex. We didn't
have a lot of money. In fact, I'll never forget what Mom told
me when she bought me a hockey stick.

"Don't break it," she said. "We can't afford another one."

She was delighted, years later, when I was accepted at
Queen's University in Kingston, Ontario. She had always
hoped I would enter a profession.

However, like many young people, I didn't know *which*
profession I should enter. In fact, I didn't have a clue what I
wanted to do. I had broad interests and a short attention span.
I lacked focus. I didn't spend a lot of time thinking about my
future. Most of my buddies were going into accounting, so

I interviewed at all the major accounting firms, too. Every single one of them turned me down flat.

I'll never forget the advice Patrick O'Neill of Price-Waterhouse gave me when I interviewed with him.

"Listen," he said, "do yourself and the profession a favor and don't go into accounting. You just don't fit this profession."

I heard him, in one respect, because I did abandon that search. But I didn't hear what he was saying about the importance of fit. I wish I had.

One night before graduation a bunch of us were sitting in the Queen's Pub. Someone in our group said, "I hear Wood Gundy is hiring." I had never heard of the company but decided to call. When I got an appointment, I prepared for the interview … by borrowing a suit.

During the interview I flew by the seat of my borrowed pants. I was delighted when they asked me to stay for the rest of the day, and even more delighted when they hired me shortly thereafter.

My Rise

That was in 1977, the beginning of a rollercoaster ride with more ups than downs and more lessons learned than regrets.

Initially, I fit the investment banking culture. Investment

banking firms were run privately by partners. Their focus was on making money for each other. These firms tended to be smaller, with flatter organizational structures, and they therefore had a greater bandwidth for tolerating different personalities—my rather brash and aggressive one included.

However, that was before the late-1980s big bang in the United Kingdom—and shortly after that the little bang in Canada—when governments in these countries allowed banks to purchase investment firms. In our case, a major corporation became our dancing partner in 1988. And just in the nick of time, too, because we were going broke.

But talk about different cultures!

In contrast to the partnership culture described above, banks are large multinational corporations managing a trust that they're handing on to future generations—the public shareholders who own them. Decisions can be made quickly in small companies, but in large corporations they are made slowly and carefully, based on a broader horizon of research, strategizing, and implementation.

In small firms, the barriers to entry are much lower, and there is usually a lot more mobility. The leader of a small partnership leads the organization by the grace and goodwill of the partners. He can be replaced at any time. Large organizations are more complex. The CEO of a large organization is like a top general in the army. He sets the goals and his decisions cascade right down through the ranks with everyone falling into line.

When these two cultures merged, none of us on the Wood Gundy side expected to last long with our new owners. Some left for other jobs on their own or were laid off. I actually lasted longer in the new environment than I thought I would. I continued to be accepted, for two reasons.

First, my financial contribution was high. I was known as a business builder and a finder and developer of talent. I was also known as someone who was willing to push the envelope to expand businesses.

And second, the investment firm and the bank were initially run as two companies. Ironically, I was a strong voice for running the two as one company, a process that actually turned the spotlight on my lack of fit.

Coming from the essentially flat hierarchy of a partnership, I didn't know how to act as you rise higher and higher in a large corporation's more vertical hierarchy.

My Fall

By the early 1990s I had helped integrate the trading rooms of Wood Gundy and CIBC. We were the first to do that anywhere in the world. So it took awhile for that spotlight to turn.

In fact, I was appointed president of Wood Gundy in 1992, at the age thirty-seven—the youngest person to be named president of a global banking unit.

Shortly after becoming president, I wrote a major strategy paper on how to grow the bank outside Canada. The key, I said, was to build Derivatives and High Yield on a global basis. I was sent to New York City in 1993 to do just that.

In less than a year, we went from a handful of people to over four hundred. My boss thanked me for finding so many talented people and getting the organization fully operational so quickly. He told me he appreciated how he could give me a tough job and know I'd do whatever it took to figure it out and make a success of it.

Once the New York operation was up and running, with the best people in place, it no longer required my day-to-day involvement. I was called back to Toronto.

As I re-entered the Toronto scene, I knew in my heart of hearts that I was in a vulnerable position. I was a change agent who had fundamentally restructured the way we did business. Thrusting so much change on the organization was causing consternation on the part of people who were feeling displaced as the organization grew differently. I sensed a lot of static around me but tried to keep my head down and keep charging ahead with what I believed was best for the company.

On Wednesday morning, June 12, 1996, I was asked to meet with my boss early in the afternoon. My spider senses told me something was wrong.

I called my wife from my office. I wasn't sure why I was telling her this, but I said, "Honey, I think I'm going to be fired this afternoon."

"Don't be ridiculous," she laughed. "You've done a great job in the U.S."

Maybe she was right, I remember thinking. After all, I had made it in New York. Wasn't that supposed to mean I could make it anywhere?

The meeting was short and not so sweet. My services were no longer needed. I did not fit.

Before I knew what had hit me, I was standing outside on Bay Street, blinking in the bright sunshine. Finance people of every stripe were returning to their offices after late lunches. Couriers were whooshing past me with messages for people in corner suites like the one I had just occupied. And there I was, after nineteen years of hard work and a long list of significant contributions, on my own and without a job.

Once the initial shock wore off, I felt pretty good. I took six months off to deprogram. As that period ended, I interviewed for a senior position in a different bank, not realizing that I was stepping into another situation where I was completely the wrong fit. I lasted two years in this position before I was back out on Bay Street blinking in the sunlight again. So I tried a completely different strategy and co-founded a financial start-up company. That company was run by a team of people who just didn't fit well with one another. It fell apart a few years later.

The loss of three major jobs in five years was a major hit not only to my ego but also to my wallet. I had never experienced stress and pressure like this. I had to find a job, and fast. I had an ex-wife, a new wife, and six kids—one of whom was very ill. I had no time to absorb the shock, take a hard look at myself, and make strategic decisions. I begged people for a job, in any capacity. I was like a falling market that was constantly testing for new lows. I kept wondering, "Is *this* rock bottom?"

A Cold, Hard Look

It soon became clear to me that I had zero prospects. I couldn't get jobs I was *overqualified* for. I kept asking myself why companies that *needed* people like me didn't *want* a person like me.

The whole experience forced me to take myself apart and put myself together again. I had to take responsibility for everything that had happened. No one was to blame but me. I knew that. I had to figure out what had happened to me and why and what I should do next. Doing that was my responsibility, too. I began to see that the way people saw me was by default, not design. I had never thought about making sure people saw me the right way. In fact, I never cared what people thought of me. So many people in business say the same thing. This is nothing other than pride, and pride goeth before a fall.

I can tell you I went through quite an agonizing—and enlightening—process to put Humpty Dumpty together again, a process that led me to my present work as a trusted advisor helping others find their job and career fit. In the rest of this book, I will help you take yourself apart. I will help you put yourself together again. I will help you ask and answer questions that will revolutionize your career and your life.

Today, I thoroughly enjoy every single day of my work. I have never been happier or more fulfilled.

I believe it won't be long before you'll be saying the same.

Video link: You've read the chapter. Now see Jim online so he can help you work through the content of this chapter. Join him at:

www.beqajinternational.com/perfectemployer

WHAT DO YOU ENJOY DOING MOST?

IF YOU LOVE WHAT YOU DO, YOU WILL
NEVER WORK A DAY IN YOUR LIFE.

Chinese proverb

JACK CAME TO MY OFFICE RECENTLY. HE couldn't understand why he hadn't been given a job he had applied for.

"You say your interview went well, but didn't you realize the interviewer had to go to her boss for the final decision?" I asked.

"Yes," he said.

"What ammunition did you give her for that conversation with her boss?"

"I gave her my résumé—plus she knows I'm the right guy."

"So you were counting on her to communicate why you're the right guy, yet you didn't give her any clear and succinct reasons *why* you're the right guy?"

I went on to explain that his chances were slim to none unless he could articulate two or three things that he was good at and make sure the interviewer was able to repeat them.

That's true for you, too. When you're asked, "What are you good at?" the answer should be on the tip of your tongue. You can't rely on someone else to figure it out. You have to hand it to them, arming them with the right message to deliver to others.

I asked this question—"What are you good at?"—of a woman who came to see me about finding a new career.

When she didn't answer right away, I said, "What are you going to lead off with in your interview? How are you going to tell them the value you can bring to the company?"

"I don't really have a pitch," she said after a few moments. "I have a résumé."

She was very well dressed, so I asked her, "Would you go to a meeting not looking your best? Relying on your résumé is like going into the interview in the wrong clothes. Your résumé is not you. It tells an interviewer nothing about what you're good at, who you work best with, how you can bring value to them."

I discovered the inadequacy of a résumé for myself when I was pounding the pavement to find a job—*any* job—after I lost three senior positions. My résumé certainly did not prevent prospective employers from seeing me as the guy who had scaled the mountain and then fallen from grace, all the way down to "unemployable."

"Jim, how would I explain to the board that I had hired

someone who had been fired from *two* top bank jobs?" the CEO of one of the banks asked me.

That was when I began to understand my challenge: coming up with a clear and compelling description of who I was and what I did best.

The purpose of this chapter is to help you set your résumé aside and take a closer look at yourself so you can begin to present yourself powerfully, positively, and accurately. The question I want to help you answer is, "What am I good at?"

Your Best and Worst Days

To answer this question, reflect first on what you enjoy doing most. This question is a great place for you to start, because most people are good at the things they enjoy doing.

Close your eyes and think about the days at work that really rocked. The days that went by in a whir because you thoroughly enjoyed everything you did. The days where you thought, on your way home, "If I could do what I did today for the rest of my career, I would be so happy."

Now think about the days that really sucked. The days that went on for an eternity because you had to do something you hated. The days where you thought, on your way home, "There's not enough gold in Fort Knox to pay me to do *that* again."

I asked Carol, who was in equity sales, to tell me the most enjoyable and memorable event of her career. I expected her to say something like the day she sold $25 million in shares of XYZ Company and received a big commission. But she didn't. She said it was updating her international clients on how the market was likely to be impacted by the election of Barack Obama as President of the United States.

As we continued to work through my process, she discovered her most enjoyable activities were providing her clients with analyses of events and economic trends so they could make better-informed investment decisions. She loved the analytical work involved in these activities.

What she liked doing, and was good at, had little to do with the job she was in and the jobs she thought she should apply for. As a result of her new insight, instead of looking for equity sales jobs because that's what she knew and they paid more money, she found a job in equity research.

What triggered her change? Looking back and figuring out what she was good at based on figuring out what she enjoyed doing the most.

Your Personal Balance Sheet

There's a simple way for you to generate a list of what you're good at. Write down a list of your best and worst days at work.

To get started, look at figure 2.1, where I list my best and worst days. Then put your list together, using figure 2.2. (This is the first of several Personal Balance Sheet™ exercises I will be taking you through. You may wish to use blank sheets of your own for this and the rest of the exercises in this book.)

FIGURE 2.1—PERSONAL BALANCE SHEET: JIM'S BEST DAYS/WORST DAYS

BEST DAYS:

- Coming up with an innovative way to increase air conditioning rentals for a company where I worked one summer
- Hiring a long list of excellent people for CIBC Woody Gundy
- Getting a strategy working for integrating the trading rooms
- Being the architect and builder of several strategy papers for the Fixed Income business
- Being the architect and builder of the strategy and plan for Derivatives and High Yield globally
- Working and living in New York

WORST DAYS:

- Wading through details to prove a case to people who played devil's advocate
- Preparing detailed presentations and defending them unsuccessfully
- Working my way through layers of the organization to reach a decision maker
- Working in a place where performance is not one of the top three criteria for success

FIGURE 2.2—PERSONAL BALANCE SHEET: YOUR BEST DAYS/WORST DAYS

BEST DAYS:

WORST DAYS:

Following are some questions that will help you get started on filling out the "best days" part of your list.

FIGURE 2.3—POSITIVE EXPERIENCES

What was the very best event at any job that you can remember (e.g., won an award; gave a speech; hired someone; led a team; completed a big project; attended an off-site retreat, business conference, annual meeting, team meeting; received special recognition).

- **When did you feel you had made a significant contribution?**
- **When did you feel most appreciated for something you had done?**
- **What do you love to do—your passion (hobby, a sport, reading)? Don't overlook things that might be turned into profitable work**

Go back to what you loved in high school or university, then the first job you had out of school, and work your way forward. Don't forget summer jobs. If your best days were when you made a lot of money, add them to your list. If your best days were when you worked for four hours, put that down; that's part of the real you.

One of my operating principles is: There is no right or wrong, good or bad; just reality. What is, is. What people are, they are. You are who you are. What matters is that you, and others, *know* who you really are. Be as straightforward and honest as you can be as you make your list.

That goes for the negative part of the sheet, too. List the unpleasant or even hated things you remember. (For examples of negative experiences, see figure 2.4.)

When you're coming up with your worst days, think about the people or tasks you avoided. Put them on your list. (Avoidance is easier these days. In fact, thank God for call display. We used to have to answer the phone to know who was calling us. Now, when we see their names flash on our telephone screens, we can be "away from our desk.")

Try this thought experiment. Imagine that you have just been given a whole new set of responsibilities at work. If one of your first thoughts was, "Good, then that means I don't have to do *x, y, and z* anymore"—what would *x, y, and z* be?

FIGURE 2.4—NEGATIVE EXPERIENCES

- **What projects or events made you uncomfortable?**
- **What did you dislike doing?**
- **What did you dread doing?**
- **What did you hate doing?**

Look at what made you unhappy—the days when you said, "I don't want to go to work" and the things you just couldn't motivate yourself to do. Don't feel guilty about not liking something; just record what it was.

When you finish listing your positive and negative activities, tasks, and experiences, look for the common denominators: the highlights representing what you enjoyed doing most and the "lowlights" representing what you hated.

THE CONNECTION BETWEEN ENJOYMENT AND SKILLS

If you're like most people I've coached through this exercise, looking at what you enjoy doing will help you encapsulate what you're good at doing.

Why? Because *most of us are good at the things we like to do.* Of course there are exceptions. You may like singing but send people running when you strike up a tune. You may like playing golf but endanger the public with every swing. There's a litmus test for these things. Ask yourself whether anyone would pay you to do what you love. If no one would pay you to sing on Broadway or to play on the PGA Tour, then leave these items off your good-at list.

One of my best days was the day at Wood Gundy when I completed a recruiting project, hiring Mike Rulle and a team of four from Lehman Brothers, who, together, were going to change the way we did business and increase our revenue more than ten-fold. When I stood up to welcome them at a special dinner, I felt as if I had assembled a team to climb Mt. Everest. (And they did make it to the top.)

I listed this on my Personal Balance Sheet, along with the types of people I had hired and who had made a difference.

This exercise helped me summarize my most enjoyable efforts: I had hired over nine hundred people and most of them had turned out to be good fits. I finally realized what the common denominator was.

My greatest satisfaction came from finding the right people for the right job. That's what I loved doing. My greatest skill was discovering talented people and putting them in jobs that benefitted them and the organization. Most of these people had succeeded where I had placed them. That told me I was good judge of talent.

The same things kept popping up when I did this Personal Balance Sheet exercise and thought about different periods in my life, whether they had to do with jobs during high school and university or on Bay Street.

It's uncanny how early we show what our skills are—sometimes long before we have developed them.

One of my summer jobs was at a company that rented out air conditioners. Two weeks in I told the owner I thought we could improve the business.

"Most of our potential customers work nine to five and are not home during the day when we call on them," I said. "They don't get home until after five p.m."

"Yeah," he said, "but we close at five."

I recommended that we hire some guys like me who were willing to work evenings. We would come in at three p.m., get the trucks ready, and call on people from five until ten.

The owner went along with my idea. I hired guys who enjoyed sales and didn't mind hard work. Then I set up the new schedule and procedures. The company had its best summer ever.

This was a strong, positive job memory for me. The job was both fulfilling and a reflection of what I was good at.

Three common denominators kept coming up in the jobs I listed as positive experiences:

- I liked doing the job
- There was an openness to new ideas

- I could figure out how to match the right people with the right jobs

As I went through the Personal Balance Sheet process, I began to see that I was a restless agent of change. No matter what I looked at, I tried to figure out how it could work better. The traits that fed this were curiosity, imagination, and an outgoing personality (some would say aggressive). I not only was a fix-it kind of guy, I believed if it wasn't broken, then break it and make it better.

As a teenager flipping burgers in the family restaurant, I suggested changes that would bring us more business. However, everyone thought I was too young to know such things. I put up with the frustration until I left.

These same traits were instrumental later in my rise at Wood Gundy. I started in Money Markets and was consistently allowed to make changes to improve the business and expand the business. Before long, profits were soaring, even though the markets were volatile. Many people were content with the status quo of the business, but it was simply impossible for me to feel that way.

Supporting Evidence

Just knowing what you're good at is not enough, however. You need to be able to give supporting evidence, too. (This point will also come into play later in the book when we discuss developing your Personal Infomercial.)

Take out another sheet of paper and write down *concrete examples* of the things you have done—things that *demonstrate* what you're good at. Examples from my career experience, in figure 2.5 below, will help you get started in filling out figure 2.6 below for yourself. List what you're good at and the accomplishments that support what you're saying.

How These Exercises Help

Here's an example of how powerful these exercises can be.

Frank, a client of mine, struggled for years to figure out what he wanted to do. When he came to see me, he was a lawyer in a big law firm. While he loved "doing the law," he hated prospecting for new business. That was a big problem, because finding new business is the number-one priority of law firms. No new business equals no billable hours.

When we sat down together, Frank said he had tried everything to become a good cold caller but it just wasn't him.

Working through his Personal Balance Sheet exercises, Frank identified that he was good at dealing with financial crises. He thrived on dealing with boards, banks, creditors, financial specialists, and their numerous legal firms. Clearly, he was a top-notch legal mind who could handle a myriad of financial problems.

I asked him three questions:

- What are some examples of what you have done well?
- What do these examples say about you?
- What can you do for companies that you love doing and that they would be willing to pay for?

As he answered these questions, Frank realized he could present himself as the go-to guy in the legal industry for companies in financial trouble. As for evidence to support this description of himself, he could point to many jobs he had done for his law firm helping turn troubled companies around. For example, he had recently been seconded to a company in severe distress and had succeeded in pulling it out of the financial fire.

When Frank was clear on what he enjoyed doing, what he was good at, and what somebody would pay him for, he was able to see potential matches. We will see, in chapter five, how he fared.

FIGURE 2.5—PERSONAL BALANCE SHEET: EVIDENCE SUPPORTING JIM'S "GOOD AT" LIST

GOOD AT:

- Good judge of how and where people fit
- Good at looking at a business and figuring out why it's not working and finding strategic ways to improve things
- Good at developing people (coaching and mentoring)

EVIDENCE:

- Improved the performance of an air conditioning business
- Hired over nine hundred people during career
- Architect and builder of new strategies for money market, the trading room, global fixed income, derivatives, and high yield
- Recruited and mentored many successful people

FIGURE 2.6—PERSONAL BALANCE SHEET: EVIDENCE SUPPORTING YOUR "GOOD AT" LIST

GOOD AT:

EVIDENCE:

Summarize Your Findings

Now pull your Personal Balance Sheet information together and summarize your three strongest "good at" points. Your summary will provide you with the content you need later for scripting your Personal Infomercial.

Take a look at my summary in figure 2.7 below to get started in filling out your summary (figure 2.8).

Practice writing your three key points. You could even corral a friend or two into letting you rehearse the lines with them as if they were interviewers.

In the chapter that follows, I'm going take you through a process similar to the one you've just been through in this chapter. The question you'll be asking is, "Who do I work best with?" Your answer to this question will lead you to a better understanding of how you're wired.

FIGURE 2.7— JIM'S PERSONAL BALANCE SHEET SUMMARY STATEMENT

- I'm a good judge of how people fit. I can summarize and categorize human talent (by personality types and characteristics) accurately and figure out where a person would fit, according to culture and company situation. My ability to do this comes from experience and an innate ability to understand people, which in turn comes from a genuine enjoyment of people

- I'm good at seeing things from a different perspective. I like to figure things out and find a better way to do them, particularly business situations that need fixing. (Or don't but could still be improved.) My way of thinking looks beyond the obvious. When a boss trusts me and gives me the scope to take on a project, I thrive and produce excellent results

- I'm good at coaching and helping people develop their skills and careers. I am genuinely interested in people. I get satisfaction from helping them. I'm able to help people decode themselves and understand themselves better. I'm also good at motivating people and mobilizing large groups to complete a task

Figure 2.8—Your Personal Balance Sheet Summary Statement

Fit Factor Tips

- In assessing yourself, there is no right or wrong, good or bad; just reality. What is, is. You are who you are. What matters is that you, and others, know who you really are and how you can add value
- You are not your résumé. It is simply a historical document— a job itinerary—of where you've worked. It's not going to lead you to the right fit
- Your Personal Balance Sheet lists will help you find the common denominators in the things you enjoy the most and least, are good at and are not good at
- Provide evidence that demonstrates your three strongest "good ats"
- Practice writing them down, in paragraph form

Video link: You've read the chapter. Now see Jim online so he can help you work through the exercises. Join him at: **www.beqajinternational.com/perfectemployer**

WHO DO YOU WORK BEST WITH, AND WHY?

DIFFICULT OR EASY, PLEASANT OR BITTER,
YOU ARE THE SAME YOU.

Martial Epigrammata

I N THE PREVIOUS CHAPTER, WE EXPLORED THE SIMPLE
but powerful question of what you're good at. You were
able to answer that question for yourself by listing the
tasks and responsibilities you enjoyed most and least.

This chapter explores your wiring—your personality. You
will be able to understand *this* topic by asking yourself, "Who
do I work best with?" Or, more precisely, "Why do I like working with those people the most?"

The answers to the two main questions of the previous
chapter and this chapter are strategically related. How so?

- The "what am I good at" question helps you determine
  the companies that *need* you
- The "who do I work best with" question will help you
  narrow that list down to the companies that also *want*

you, because they are populated by the kind of people you're most compatible with

I discovered the importance of this second question when I was running around scattering my résumé like seed on any patch of grass I could find. I started to realize that lots of companies needed me but none of them *wanted* me.

That forced me to examine the personalities of those I worked well with or poorly with. Then I asked myself why I worked well with some and not others. What were the characteristics of these different types of people? What were *my* characteristics?

Personality Differences

If I had known more about personality differences earlier, I would have taken a pass on a job I was offered shortly after my fall from the heights of the bank. Because I did not have this knowledge in hand, I blew past several signs that were screaming at me to flee.

First, my future boss smoked at his desk during my interview, in spite of the company's and the building's no-smoking policy.

Second, he sat there reconciling his cancelled checks against his checkbook. Hell, I don't even know where my checkbook *is*, much less whether it's balanced. Someone that detail-conscious was going to drive me crazy (and vice versa).

And third, when I said I couldn't start right away because of a scheduled trip with the boys to Las Vegas, he trotted out a sermon on the stupidity of wasting money on the gaming tables. But I *love* trips to Las Vegas!

Don't get me wrong. I liked this man. We played golf together. I'm not in any way saying my personality characteristics are good and his bad. I'm saying they were different. Two people on opposite sides of the personality fence were doomed to work poorly together.

I had always assumed you worked with the people you worked with. That when you were hired by an organization, you got what you got. Now that I was on the outside looking in, I thought, "Athletes think about the teams they would prefer to play on—why couldn't I look for the people I want to work with, too?"

The point is for you to find a place to work not just because it's a job you can do or that pays well but because the job gives off strong signals of fit, given what you now know more clearly about yourself. And one of the critical pieces of your self-knowledge is to ask whether a company is filled with people you would like to work with.

Following, in figure 3.1, is a list of the kinds of people I work well with and those I don't. It is followed by a page, figure 3.2, for you to fill out.

FIGURE 3.1—PERSONAL BALANCE SHEET: JIM'S WORK BEST WITH/ WORK WORST WITH LIST

JIM WORKS BEST WITH:

- People who rely on me to be the architect of a plan and to execute the plan
- People who give me plenty of bandwidth
- People who are able to see something is broken and know something has to change
- People who trust me and are willing to delegate the responsibility to me to get it done

JIM WORKS WORST WITH:

- Micromanagers
- People who won't even consider a big-picture approach to solving a problem
- People who deal with conflicts by yelling
- People who create policies and procedures they don't follow themselves

FIGURE 3.2—PERSONAL BALANCE SHEET: YOUR WORK BEST WITH/ WORK WORST WITH LIST

WORK BEST WITH

-
-
-
-

WORK WORST WITH

-
-
-
-

YOUR WIRING

Wiring? What's that? The reason we work better with some people than others is that we're all wired differently. Our wiring has to do with things we're good at. Things we like. People we like. Things and people we *don't* like.

Our wiring is a combination of genetics, birth order, environment, and our personal history—the choices we've made, the relationships we've had, and the relationships we're in right now.

Some of us are wired for detail, mathematics, and analytical thinking and others for creativity, spatial design, and music. Some are the strong silent type; others are outgoing and spontaneous. We cannot change our basic wiring. Introverts can't turn themselves into extroverts. Messy types can't transform themselves into neatness freaks. And that's okay.

The information you're compiling about yourself is essentially a record of your strengths. As you continue to go through the process of this book, recognize your weaknesses—that's very important—but focus on your strengths. Don't make the mistake of ignoring your wiring and trying to improve on the things you're *not* good at. It's much more strategic to concentrate on, and build on, the things you *are* good at.

You've got to lead with your strengths. I'm always making this point to my kids.

"Don't bust your chops trying to be adequate at something you're not wired for," I tell them. "Spend your time expanding on the things you're really good at. Deal from strength."

If you're like most people, you find it difficult to articulate your strengths. Perhaps that's because you're too close to yourself to see them. Or maybe because it was drilled into you as a child that you're not supposed to brag. However, being able to state your strengths is key to everything else when it comes to hiring the perfect employer.

WHAT'S YOUR PERSONALITY TYPE?

You don't have to be a psychologist to figure out your personality type. You can take various tests administered by psychologists. You can even take some of them online. I have found the Myers-Briggs Type Indicator test to be very helpful. (Visit our website www.beqajinternational.com for links to Myers-Briggs and other online tests.)

I'm going to go into just enough detail about the Myers-Briggs test to make a point about personality differences.

This test analyzes two contrasting preferences related to various aspects of personality. You can get a good start on defining your personality type just by writing down the letters that apply to you as you answer the following questions (for example, E for Extroversion or I for Introversion, S for Sensing or N for Intuition, and so on):

1. Extroversion (E) or Introversion (I):
   Do you prefer to focus on the outer world or on your own inner world?
2. Sensing (S) or Intuition (N):
   Do you prefer to focus on the basic information you take in or do you prefer to interpret and add meaning?
3. Thinking (T) or Feeling (F):
   When making decisions, do you prefer to first look at logic and consistency or first look at the people and special circumstances?
4. Judging (J) or Perceiving (P):
   In dealing with the outside world, do you prefer to get things decided or do you prefer to stay open to new information and options?

I took the more detailed test and came out with the profile of an ENFP (Extroverted, Intuitive, Feeling, Perceiving). This was a eureka moment for me because I finally understood why I don't work well with micromanagers.

In the Myers-Briggs scheme of things, micromanager sorts often measure up as ISTJs (Introverted, Sensing, Thinking, Judging). I now could see that:

- An ISTJ's **S** trait (Sensing: focusing on facts, details, data collection) clashes with my **N** trait (Intuitive: seeing the big picture and future possibilities)
- An ISTJ's **J** trait (Judging: rational, logical, planned, orderly) clashes with my **P** trait (Perceiving: going with the flow, spontaneous, flexible)

HOW KNOWING YOUR PERSONALITY HELPS

It's amazing how my understanding of the world of work opened up when I understood my personality better. My main takeaway was that I should not work *for* ISTJs, and that I should develop coping mechanisms when I needed to work *with* them.

It's not that I can't be detailed, especially when the subject is of real interest to me. It's just that as an ENFP I am not *oriented* that way. I'm not good at presenting a message to ISTJs in the form and detail they need in order to understand and accept it. I've tried and tried. I've found it's best if I can delegate that level of detail to others.

For example, although I understand finance and accounting, I sometimes prevent a frustrating conversation with my accountant by saying, "You do the detail work and then give me your recommendation and supporting evidence."

Other times I delegate a more detail-oriented person to act as a buffer for me. I may say to that same accountant, "I'd like you to work with so-and-so on the details and summarize them for me so I can work with them on the final decision."

It's critical for everyone to understand that individuals should not try to turn others into their type. When managers try to change the personality type of their reports, or when members of a team try to do the same with other members, the only thing that results is dysfunctionality.

For me to tell an ISTJ, "Don't worry about the numbers ..." will not work. In turn, an ISTJ should not make me come to meetings armed to the teeth with data and analyses. We should figure out which meetings I really need to attend. And when I'm in those meetings, I should be given the freedom to report on the big picture instead of on each and every individual brushstroke.

Today in my business I focus on where I can have the highest probability of success. I know I'm not for everybody. I seek out clients I'm compatible with: clients who see me as a trusted advisor and collaborative partner.

"We're not for you," I once told a prospective client, a CEO.

He was surprised. He said no service provider had ever told him that before.

I knew the fit was not right. I live this way now in everything I do, with every client I consider and with each one I take on. I've found that *there's nothing more rewarding than being authentic to how you are wired and who you really are.*

Compatibility Is Not Sameness

Compatibility in the workplace does not mean everyone has to have the same wiring. On the contrary, you *want* diversity. Companies work best when they are staffed with a complement of personality types. Compatibility isn't sameness; it means everyone works well together.

Your friends are not all of the same personality type, yet you are attracted to them. There is something at their core that makes you feel comfortable. You make accommodations for the differences and adapt. Compatibility is about fit, not about being the same.

As an ENFP (Extroverted, Intuitive, Feeling, Perceiving), I am somewhat different from an ENTP (Extroverted, Intuitive, Thinking, Perceiving). We will disagree on how we might do something, but we are compatible in several very important ways: We both like to think about the big picture. We're both flexible. We both enjoy brainstorming and exploring possibilities.

We complement each other because I look at the big picture from the people perspective while she looks at the big picture from the rational and analytical perspective.

Think of yourself as a matchmaker. You're going to be married to a job and career for a long time. You're looking for the highest possible level of compatibility in order to achieve the highest probability of success. This search for compatibility is a continuous one. You will have to readjust your working style every time there's a change in your job or working relationships.

Chapter six will help you in more detail to find what I call your Target Rich Environment: companies that need what you're good at and that are populated by the type of people you work best with. You don't want to take a job in a place you think is collegial only to find out it's full of competitive, dog-eat-dog types.

There's nothing wrong with a competitive and aggressive approach. However, if you're introverted and judging, you need time to organize your thoughts and come to your conclusions. The last place you want to be is a knock 'em down, drag 'em out environment of extroverts who act first and think later.

INTERVIEW THE INTERVIEWER

Ask questions during your interview to figure out whether the company is made up of the sort of people you're compatible with. This is especially important when it comes to your direct superiors. (The company should be looking at you in this way, too, but don't count on it. Take responsibility for doing this detective work yourself.)

During interviews and meet-and-greet sessions, look around the organization and talk to as many people as possible.

Don't make your judgment based solely on your perception of the interviewer, however. He or she may not be typical of the firm's workforce. Get information from people outside the company, as well. You can learn a lot from a company's customers or even its suppliers. It's easier than you think. Start with a visit to the company's website and then make a few telephone calls.

Charlene, a young woman I coached, is a good example of this kind of detective work. She had worked for three years in sales with two difficult bosses.

"They micro-managed me, gave me menial tasks, and made it pretty clear they didn't like working with women," was her summary. "And I hated the rote work I had to do preparing spreadsheets for presentations."

It was a toxic environment and so she left. I walked her through my process. She identified what she liked doing, what she was good at, the evidence that supported what she was good at, and the type of people she worked best with.

What set Charlene apart was her commitment to perform due diligence. She assessed potential companies and asked friends and friends of friends what they thought and knew. She talked to over forty people during her search for the right fit.

"I had conversations with anybody who would talk to me and met with people who worked in those companies or were connected to those industries. I focused on people my age. I bought a lot of cups of coffee for people. It was worth it."

Charlene ended up in a company where she wanted to be: a place with a high level of compatibility with how she is wired.

Be sure to tell interviewers the kind of people you work best with. Ask whether those types of people work in the prospective company. Listen for words like collegial, easygoing, family-like, buttoned down, hard-driving, very competitive, no-nonsense, what the boss says goes.

As you listen to the interviewer's responses, ask: Why is it this way? How widespread is it?

If the interviewer doesn't offer any information, you can use certain phrases to extract what you need to know. For example, it's quite appropriate to say: "Tell me a little about what it's like to work here: Is it laid-back or very competitive?" Following are the types of questions to ask.

- Is it all business and no fun?
- Is it the boss's way or the highway?
- Is there much independence?
- Do you get support from upper management?
- Is it collegial and easygoing?
- Is there a family-like atmosphere?

You can also achieve your objective by how you answer the interviewer's questions. When she says, "What exactly do you want to do?" Or "What type of job are you looking for?" you can say:

- I know that wherever I work, the things I want to be doing are (*fill in your specifics*)
- These are the kind of people I'm looking to work with (*fill in specifics*)
- I want to make sure that I'm in a place that is (*fill in specifics*)

You'll be surprised by how forthcoming interviewers will be. People like to talk about themselves and about their company's organizational culture and people. You simply have to develop a clear view of what you're looking for and arm yourself with the right questions.

Fit Factor Tips

- Knowing yourself includes knowing who you enjoy working with, and why. This will help you see how you're wired. Knowing how you are wired will help you find the right fit
- Consider taking one of the easy-to-do online tests (e.g., Myers-Briggs). Refer to other books and resources
- List your main characteristics
- Study and know the general characteristics of the type of people you're compatible and incompatible with
- Compatibility doesn't mean everyone's the same; it means you fit
- Look to find a company and people where your personality type will be a good fit
- *Your* needs, not their needs, are what matter. You are interviewing them as much as they are interviewing you

Video link: You've read the chapter. Now see Jim online so he can help you work through the exercises. Join him at: **www.beqajinternational.com/perfectemployer**

What's Your Preferred Method for Resolving Conflicts?

YOUR REAL WORLD IS A GIANT NEGOTIATING TABLE,
AND LIKE IT OR NOT, YOU'RE A PARTICIPANT.

Herb Cohen

MOST PEOPLE DON'T EVEN THINK OF ASKING A prospective employer how people in the company resolve conflicts. It's an important question, however, because your search for compatibility, which we discussed in the previous chapter, cannot be complete unless you know whether there's an alignment between your preferred style of resolving conflicts and the predominant style of the company.

After all, there's no such thing as a job without conflicts. And conflicts over the way conflicts are handled can end up being worse than the conflicts themselves.

But do you actually know your preferred style of resolving conflicts? Most of us can't say what it is without a little bit of thinking.

Let's say you hate hearing people scream and yell. How will you fare if your new boss starts each day by tearing a strip off someone just to get his juices flowing? Or starts every meeting with a tirade just to clear the air?

Or let's say you like to get conflict out in the open. Are you going to be happy working for a company where people avoid conflicts most of the time?

Let's say you prefer dealing with conflicts by collaborating with others toward a solution. When you find a company that takes this approach, you may well be in what I'll describe in the next chapter as your Target Rich Environment. This is a company worth considering.

I first spotted differences in conflict-resolution styles in the late 1980s when investment firms, including mine, were being purchased by banks. I saw that, for the most part, people on the investment firm side liked to deal with conflict straight on. We dealt with them competitively. Resolution came when a clear winner emerged. People in the banks preferred to handle conflict more slowly, through consensus building and compromise.

The approaches themselves are neither right nor wrong. The question is whether your style is compatible with the main style of the company you're considering. Knowledge is power. You want to steer clear of jobs where your approach is diametrically opposed to that of the majority of the people who work there. (Ideally, organizations would be sensitive in their hiring guidelines to differences in conflict-resolution styles and turn job seekers away if their approach is not a fit with theirs. Don't count on it, though; it's your responsibility to know your style and figure out theirs.)

DETECTING CONFLICT-RESOLUTION STYLES

Various tools are available to help you understand the conflict-resolution approach or approaches you prefer to use. One of the best I've come across is Kenneth W. Thomas and Ralph H. Kilmann's Conflict Mode Instrument (known as the TKI). You can take a basic self-scoring exercise on the website www.KilmannDiagnostics.com to determine what your mode is. The exercise takes about fifteen minutes to complete.

The TKI measures your behavior in terms of how assertive or cooperative it is. Then it measures your predominant mode of conflict resolution. There are five main modes, according to Kilmann Diagnostics:

(1) **Competing**: Kilmann Diagnostics says this term describes people who are "assertive and uncooperative." People who pursue their own concerns at the expense of others.

Competing types use whatever power they have to stand up for their rights or defend their position. Sometimes their only concern is to win.

(2) **Accommodating**: This describes people who are "unassertive and cooperative." People of this style are the opposite of competing types. They will sacrifice their concerns for the sake of others. Their instinct is to obey or yield.

(3) **Avoiding**: People of this type are "unassertive and uncooperative." They are unlike both the competing and the accommodating types because they neither go after their own interests nor yield their interests. They try to sidestep issues or postpone them. They will sometimes withdraw completely if a situation feels threatening to them.

(4) **Collaborating**: These people are "assertive and cooperative." They try to "work with others to find some solution that fully satisfies their concerns." This may mean "digging into an issue to pinpoint the underlying needs and wants of the two individuals."

(5) **Compromising**: This describes people who are "moderate in assertiveness and cooperativeness." Such people look

for "some expedient, mutually acceptable solution that partially satisfies both parties." Compromising "gives up more than competing but less than accommodating. Likewise, it addresses an issue more directly than avoiding, but does not explore it in as much depth as collaborating."

Determining the mode you prefer and that of others is not an exact science. People may use all five approaches to one degree or another. And a lot depends on the nature of the conflict itself. However, most people, as a result of temperament and practice, use one or two modes more than the others.

Fred, a middle manager I coached, is a good example of what can happen when conflict-resolution styles clash.

Fred is a competitive guy. His attitude is: Got a problem? Let's talk. Let's solve it. And move on.

But Fred had joined a firm whose boss was fond of saying, "We're like family around here." The members of this firm didn't like confrontation. When a conflict had to be handled, they used compromise, through a long discussion or a series of meetings.

Fred lacked patience for this approach. His frustration was obvious. A couple of times he walked out on what this company called "talk-it-out meetings."

Fred's impatience was seen as intolerance, his openness as aggression, and his candor as disruptiveness. He soon enough wore out his welcome and left the firm, disillusioned.

Until he and I spoke, Fred didn't realize that the main reason for his exit was his lack of understanding about conflict resolution.

The Complexity of Conflict Resolution

Conflict resolution on the job can be a complex challenge. For example, you will be marginalized at work if you prefer to deal with conflicts straight on but most of your co-workers avoid them. Or if you fold like a cheap suitcase at the slightest ripple of tension and most of your colleagues are competitive.

As for me, I'm not interested in either overly competitive or compromising places. In competitive places it's about who wins, whether that win is good for the company or not. I find that seeking a compromise—usually to keep the majority happy—doesn't work. I am perfectly okay when someone says, "Hey Jim, the approach you're recommending sucks." My response is, "Okay, tell me why you think that." If I understand the problem, then I can then deal with it and usually work with the person to solve it.

Based on the Thomas-Kilmann modes, I predominantly use the collaborating approach. I fully expect people who know me to snort at this statement. But it's true. I like to work with people to find the right answer as opposed to finding the answer that benefits me more than others or a compromise that doesn't really benefit either side.

Seeking the right answer collaboratively can be risky. There were times at the bank, for example, when I was involved in reinventing parts of the business. I knew the changes I was making could jeopardize my personal success, but that was not my first concern. I believed the change I was heading up was best for the business.

I even said once, during a board meeting, "You know what? The strategy we're discussing is the best one for our company even though it means some of us may not be around in five years."

How true—I was one the one sent packing!

I have no trouble with people who are assertive—even aggressive—in making their case. But I can't stand it when people argue for the sake of arguing. I have trouble with the opposite situation, too: when people won't deal with things up front. When I partnered with others in a start-up company, we never resolved conflict; we constantly avoided it. Everybody talked behind everybody's back. I hate that approach. Most people do.

How to Use Your New Knowledge

Why is all of this so important? Because it will play into some important decisions you're going to be making.

Imagine you're considering an employment offer from two companies. If your decision is based solely on title, salary, and convenience, you could be in for a big surprise the first time a conflict rears its head in your new job. Better to know, before you sign on the dotted line, whether your way of resolving conflicts fits with either of the companies.

This point should come before most other considerations. If you end up in the wrong organization, you're going to hate your work. It won't matter how well the organization uses your skills or how much it pays you.

For example, consider the investment firms J.P. Morgan and Bear Stearns. They were at the opposite ends of the conflict-resolution spectrum. (I say "were" because Bear Stearns is no longer with us, courtesy of the Great Recession.)

J.P. Morgan is steeped in blue blood history. It has an old school, gentlemanly culture. J.P. Morgan people discuss the pros and cons of a situation and then bring everyone concerned together in an attempt to resolve it. Although the firm is competitive, it focuses on collaboration, accommodation, and compromise. It aims at trying to do the right thing for everyone.

Bear Stearns was the very antithesis of this. Its culture was survival of the fittest. Lots of competition and no compromise and avoidance. At Bear Stearns it was sink or swim. (They're not swimming anymore, but that is beside the point.)

If you were choosing between such firms, you would consider salary, perks, and location. But these criteria pale in comparison with their fundamental difference in how they handle conflicts.

The large consulting firm McKinsey & Company offers quite a different example. McKinsey takes a competitive *and* a collaborative approach to conflict resolution. It is a collaborative partnership. But it is also highly competitive. The basic principle is you get promoted up or you're out. If you make it to the partner level, you must maintain a certain level of contribution or you're out.

Different approaches can, and do, exist *within* many companies; it's the degree to which they are compatible with your approach that matters most. In fact, when you're interviewing at a larger company, probe for specifics about the division or department you're looking at. Conflicts may be handled differently in different parts of the company.

Asking the Conflict-Resolution Question

You can take different approaches to the conflict-resolution question in an interview.

- You can be very direct and ask, "How do you resolve conflict in this organization?"
- Or you can be more indirect and say, "Tell me a little about the boss. Is it his way or the highway?"

Your focus should first of all be on the conflict-resolution approach of the person you'll be reporting to. This person will control your livelihood. You're not in control of your peers. However, if you work for a person with a compatible style of conflict resolution, you can handle any lateral mismatches much more easily.

Also, you can actually tell the interviewer what you're looking for and turn it into several questions: "I'm pretty direct when it comes to resolving problems and conflict. How is it here? Open? Is pretty much everything on the table? Or is there a lot of a compromise and avoidance—which doesn't work for me."

A company that's right for you will respect your questions.

Conflict-Resolution Matching

Go back to your Personal Balance Sheet notes from chapters two and three. Look at the list of the people you did and didn't work well with (figure 3.2). Now add to this sheet each person's main approach to conflict resolution, using the five main styles discussed above: competing, accommodating, avoiding, collaborating, and compromising. See if a pattern emerges concerning the conflict-resolution style or styles you are most compatible with.

Narrowing Your Search

You are well on your way to hiring the perfect employer. You know how to answer three crucial questions:

- What am I good at?
- How am I wired?
- How do I prefer to resolve conflicts?

The next step, which is covered in the following chapter, is to narrow your search—in order to broaden the likelihood of your success.

Fit Factor Tips

- There are five basic approaches to conflict resolution: Competing, Accommodating, Avoiding, Collaborating, Compromising
- Take the Thomas-Kilmann Conflict Mode Instrument test (or a similar test) to determine how you prefer to resolve conflict
- Make sure the conflict-resolution culture of a prospective employer is compatible with your conflict-resolution style
- Looking back at the types of people you do and don't work best with, identify the main ways they handle conflict
- Start determining the questions you can ask in interviews to get a bead on the company's conflict-resolution style

Video link: You've read the chapter. Now see Jim online so he can help you work through the exercises. Join him at: **www.beqajinternational.com/perfectemployer**

How to Find Your Target Rich Environment

Do not labor with bigger nets,
fish where the fish are.

Greek fisherman

BEFORE I WENT THROUGH THE PROCESS OF SEARCH-ing for me, I was all over the place when looking for a job. Literally. I went here and there, pitching almost anyone in financial services where I could get my foot in the door. I handed out my résumé, pitched my skills, networked, and met with interviewer after interviewer.

But I was wasting a lot of time and effort. I could have pitched a thousand people and it wouldn't have made any dif-ference. Why? Because I wasn't looking in the right places.

The same principle applies to finding an employer that fits you. You must search within your Target Rich Environment, an environment in which your probability of success is high-est because you are both needed and wanted.

Blinding Glimpses of the Obvious

It took me awhile to figure this out. I was still focusing on getting a job instead of finding the right fit.

I remember driving back and forth several times to meet with the CEO of a mutual fund firm whose offices were outside Toronto. During one of those drives I wondered why I would want to work there, considering the joys of driving in the winter.

Of course, weather shouldn't have been a major criterion for me, but in any case I didn't get the job. I shouldn't have considered it in the first place, though. The CEO and I are opposites in our personalities. Our wiring would have short-circuited in no time.

Later I could state my value more clearly as being a trusted advisor who works best with someone who gives me a lot of scope to build a business.

Well, this man was not the type to allow me much scope. He is the founder of his company. His imprint is on most aspects of the business. Nothing wrong with that. But working there would not have been a good fit for me. He had zero interest in delegating important challenges to others and giving them the space to make a success of them.

"I want everyone in this company to think of it as their own," he said.

"You own ninety percent of the stock. How are they supposed to think that way?" was my response.

Sometimes blinding glimpses of the obvious are hard to see. That must be why they call them blinding. It's human nature to see what we have always seen or want to see. We keep going back to the same fishing hole even though we haven't caught anything there for a long time. We keep casting a bigger and bigger net in the same fishless place.

Why?

Because it's what we know. It's what we've always done. It's what we're comfortable with.

The approach may seem right, but it's all wrong. If you want to catch fish you have to fish in the most productive and richest places—in your Target Rich Environment.

Your TRE Is Not a Specific Place

Don't think of your Target Rich Environment as a place but as a concept that defines the type of work, people, company, and industry—a total environment—where you fit. Your TRE is the one in which you have the highest probability of finding an employer that fits you.

Let me re-emphasize what doesn't give you a high probability of success: scattering résumés far and wide, answering dozens of Internet postings, flitting about networking, and attending workshops.

Your focus must be on finding organizations that *fit you* based on your newly acquired wealth of knowledge about yourself. Your objective is to interview with companies that are most likely to need you, want you, and hire you.

Marketing 101 teaches us to be targeted when promoting and selling products and services. And what product and service is more valuable than you? None.

So stop pitching in places that are unsuited to you.

Remember Charlene in chapter three, who talked to more than forty people in her search for the company that fit her best? Those forty souls were not selected shotgun style. They fit her TRE. That's focused preparation.

Companies that make it into your TRE are the ones that:

(1) Need what you are good at

(2) Want you

(3) Have the same philosophy, vision, culture, as you

(4) Are staffed by people likely to be compatible with you

(5) Have a conflict-resolution process that fits you

(6) Meet your general criteria regarding size, growth, and opportunity

FINDING MY TRE

It took me too long to realize I wasn't going to get a job where I was looking. You could say I was barking up the wrong TRE. There were no jobs available to me similar to my previous ones. Senior leadership positions in the major financial institutions were either filled, or if they were open they were not open to me. That whole territory was a target *poor* environment.

Despite this, I did still want to stay in the financial services sector. So I started looking behind the banks and financial institutions at the significant group of institutions that supported them. I focused on companies in the consulting, recruiting, and coaching field—areas I had identified for me as "liking" and "good at."

My next step was to determine the specific target companies that needed my skills and wanted my personality type.

First, I drew up a long list of firms. Then I whittled the list down to the companies I thought *needed* me. Then I eliminated any companies on the list that were unlikely to *want* me, companies with:

- Compromising or avoidance cultures
- Micromanagers who were most likely ISTJs (Introverted, Sensing, Thinking, Judging)

The companies on my short list were good ones. However, I soon began to understand that even these would not be a good fit for me. From my short list, I set up a series of meetings. Not too long into the interview process, my suspicions were confirmed. Most of the organizations *needed* me—they agreed I would be a valuable asset. Some wanted me to join them. Most didn't, but that was all right. I realized that they wouldn't have been the right fit for me. It was a seminal moment for me when I realized, "Why would I want that job?"

Some of the companies that didn't *want* me gave me a number of reasons why.

- "Jim, we're a rules-based organization and you're the kind of guy who works better outside the rules"
- "We're too structured for you. You like independence and working across boundaries. We have a lot of boundaries here"
- "Jim, your ability to find great talent is unquestioned but your techniques and style wouldn't fit here. We're quite formal"

You may have heard Albert Einstein's famous definition of insanity as "doing the same thing over and over again and expecting different results." I finally got it. I no longer needed to take a job on in order to be told I didn't fit; I could detect it clearly myself, beforehand.

As mentioned, when I realized there were no first-line jobs in investment firms that fit me, I thought about companies serving the banks—recruiting, consulting, and coaching firms.

As I interviewed with these types of firms, I began to see that, without exception, none of them did what I was good at: providing a cohesive approach to consulting, recruiting, and coaching.

I thought, "This is the right ball; I've got to hit it."

I discussed my perception with some of them.

"We have consulting and we have recruiting and we have coaching," was the reply I got. "They are distinct functions within different firms. We don't get too involved in strategic issues."

"Why are they not together?" I asked.

"Well, that's not the way we do it," they replied.

The more I talked to different people and the more information I gathered, the more I saw a void in the marketplace. No one was offering a single source for what in reality are three closely related needs:

- Trusted strategic advice
- In-depth recruiting of talent
- Experienced development of people (coaching and mentoring)

My thinking was simple. If people are the most important asset in an organization (human capital), why wouldn't they be looked at holistically and linked by common thinking with regard to strategy, recruiting, and ongoing personnel development? Most firms lacked a single source with the experience, background, and skill set to deliver all three—consulting, recruiting, and coaching/mentoring—as a package, whether integrated or à la carte.

I began to see that if I could deliver this on my own, then I would be exactly where I should be: doing the three things I was good at, unencumbered by rigid structures, free of bureaucratic procedures, and able to choose the people I worked with.

Eureka!

It was the chief eureka moment of my life, let me tell you. And I had it because I knew what I was looking for, had thoroughly researched my TRE, and had done my due diligence. When I discovered there was no company that fit my TRE, I created my own. It was the best career move I ever made.

You may not be interested in building your own business, but the same principles and processes apply. You must define your TRE so you can increase your probability of finding the best place to work.

One day, shortly after I had formed my new business, I was

speaking to a long-time business acquaintance, Geoff Beattie, President and CEO of The Woodbridge Company and a director on the boards of GE, Thomson Reuters, and Royal Bank of Canada.

"Bakes," he said, "you don't realize it but you're going to have far more influence over the financial services industry now in your new career than you ever did at your previous firms."

His statement confirmed for me that I have found my TRE—clients who:

- See the value I can add
- Are open to being helped
- See me not as an expense but as part of their own strategy
- See my unorthodox personality and methods as a plus

And it's true. I *have* found the right fit for me: work in which I am achieving my goal of contributing to the betterment of people and organizations while doing what I am good at and love to do. And making money at it.

SELLING KNIVES

It's amazing how often people head in precisely the wrong direction. They want to work in an industry because they think it's what they should do. But the industry, meanwhile, simply isn't right for them.

I spoke to a class at the University of Western Ontario recently about the importance of determining and articulating what you're good in the process of finding the right fit. One of the students raised his hand.

"What you're saying is great if you've already been out there working," he said, "but how do you find your fit if you're still in school?"

To answer his question I picked someone out of the class and asked him what he was good at.

"I'm a second-year student," he said. "I don't know what I'm good at."

I asked him about his summer jobs. He said one summer he worked as an intern at a bank, another in a call centre, and another selling knives.

"Of those summer jobs, which did you enjoy doing the most?"

"Selling knives."

"Why?"

"Because I got paid daily and I knew if I put in extra time I could make extra cash. I loved cold calling and being pleasantly surprised how many people bought the knives because they recognized they were a good product. I liked working independently. If I wanted to work nights and weekends, I could. If I wanted to take a day off, I could. I liked not having a boss."

"What are you going to do when you graduate?" I asked.

"Probably go into investment banking."

"You're kidding me, aren't you? There's nothing wrong with working in that industry, and you'd probably do well at it, but you're a natural salesperson. Do you realize that less than ten percent of people like to cold call? Do you realize that very few people are willing to live by their own resources—to eat what they kill? I could see it in your eyes when you talked about selling knives. You love selling. Why wouldn't you look for work in a company like IBM or Xerox? Places with a strong sales culture that will help you hone your sales skills?"

I showed him and the rest of the students how you can determine what you're good at from what you enjoy doing most, and how that reveals the environment in which you should be looking for work.

"You're not going to be happy in a place where you're put in a box," I said to this student. "You want to work in a firm that gives you more latitude, one that's going to teach you more about the things you love doing."

This young man could have been rejected for all the right reasons but not understand why he had been rejected: that the people he had interviewed with, whether consciously or not, recognized he wasn't the right fit for them. Whereas a pharmaceutical company would love a guy like him. There would be an instant recognition, on both sides, of fit.

Frank's Target Rich Environment

Let's go back briefly to Frank. He's the lawyer I spoke of earlier, in chapter two, who thought he wanted to be a lawyer in a big law firm but discovered he was better suited to be the go-to lawyer for companies in financial crisis.

After working through his Personal Balance Sheet, Frank narrowed his Target Rich Environment down to companies that were:

- Experiencing a falling stock price and in serious financial difficulty
- Under siege by debtors
- Dealing with complex financial, legal, and creditor issues
- In danger of going bankrupt

This was a TRE that fit Frank's skills, experience, and personality. He could provide tangible value to companies in this group and be paid for it. I told him if he confined himself to searching in this TRE, he would maximize his probability of success. And he did.

Mapping Your Target Rich Environment

I'm going to show you my TRE list (figure 5.1) to get you started on writing yours (figure 5.2).

Like a sales and marketing group analyzing any target market, developing your TRE takes time. Think of it as like a funnel process. Draw up a list by starting with a relatively broad definition of the types of companies. Then narrow it down to a short list. This will take time, but it will save you time. More importantly, it will save you from landing in the wrong place.

Once you have determined your TRE, you can start selling yourself to those organizations. The following chapter shows you how to present your Personal Infomercial as part of this essential sales process.

Figure 5.1—Jim's Target Rich Environment Companies

CLIENTS THAT NEED ME (NEED MY SKILLS)

- Are interested and open to outside opinions
- Take ownership of strategic and recruiting issues versus delegating to other functions
- Are aware that they need help
- Are open to being helped
- Are open to having a trusted advisor relationship

CLIENTS FROM THE ABOVE LIST THAT WANT ME (ARE COMPATIBLE WITH ME, HAVE CONFLICT-RESOLUTION STYLES THAT MESH WITH MINE)

- Value going straight to the solution, as opposed to going through layers of decision making
- Are expanding their business
- Appreciate my unorthodox personality and approach

FIGURE 5.2—YOUR TARGET RICH
ENVIRONMENT

COMPANIES THAT NEED YOU
(NEED YOUR SKILLS)

COMPANIES FROM THE ABOVE LIST THAT WANT
YOU (ARE COMPATIBLE WITH YOU, HAVE CONFLICT-
RESOLUTION STYLES THAT MESH WITH YOURS)

Fit Factor Tips

- If you clearly define your TRE, you will dramatically increase your probability of success
- Don't think of your TRE as a place; see it as a concept that defines the type of work, people, company and industry—a total environment—in which you see a great fit for you
- Do your research and due diligence. Look into companies, ask others, and then draw up a short list of employers that are a great fit for you

Video link: You've read the chapter. Now see Jim online so he can help you work through the exercises. Join him at: **www.beqajinternational.com/perfectemployer**

How to Present Your Personal Infomercial

It's a luxury to be understood.

Ralph Waldo Emerson

EVERYTHING WE'VE DISCUSSED IN THIS BOOK HAS
been heading toward this chapter on your Personal
Infomercial. So far, through the Personal Balance
Sheet and TRE exercises, you have determined:

- What you're good at
- How you're wired
- How you prefer to resolve conflicts
- Your Target Rich Environment, a list of the companies
  that are a likely fit for you because they need you and
  want you

Now it's time for you to pull all of this together. It's time for
you to script your Personal Infomercial.

Your infomercial is a clear and compelling presentation of who you are and what you're looking for. It is:

- What you say to colleagues when you tell them you're looking for the right fit—the perfect employer to hire
- What you say to interviewers in the companies that are part of your TRE
- What your colleagues say about you when they mention you to others
- What your interviewer says when he or she recommends you for further consideration

As I have said several times, you are not your résumé. However, because most companies will ask you to submit a résumé, make sure yours leads off with your infomercial in written form. A résumé with this kind of lead-in blows other résumés out of the water. Your lead-in will also serve to reinforce the infomercial you present when your résumé is reviewed later in the process.

No matter what, though, remember that your résumé is just a supporting document. What you say to others (and what they say about you to others) is what really counts.

Simplify, Simplify

Dan, a client of mine, called me one day after he came out of a meeting with a prospective employer. I knew something was up because Dan's a low-key kind of guy and he sounded excited.

"Jim, I met with a group who are right in my TRE and the fit is good," he said. "I know it and they know it."

He went on to describe the organization.

Then he said, "You know what? The best thing about delivering my Personal Infomercial was their reaction to it. Not just the content—which they liked—but the fact that I laid out, in short order, exactly what I was good at and what I wanted. They said they'd never experienced such a direct and cogent approach."

Dan is now happily working in that new job.

It had taken Dan awhile to refine his infomercial. At first he couldn't bring himself to turn his interviewing approach into this atypical format. Like most people, he felt he had to jam everything he'd ever done into his pitch.

That was not surprising. He *had* accomplished a lot. He had already been in three careers and now, in his early fifties, he was reinventing another one.

"You don't have to say it all up front," I had told him. "The information will mean more when you frame it properly and succinctly. That will prompt interviewers to ask you for more information. You can add the details on an as-needed basis. That's very different from dumping a ton of stuff on them."

Things turned around for Dan because he:

- Went back over his Personal Balance Sheet—his notes about his skills, his personality, his compatibility issues, and his preferred conflict-resolution style
- Determined his Target Rich Environment
- Simplified his infomercial until it hit the main points

"Once I sifted through everything in my past and simplified it," Dan said, "I saw how I could communicate the core points clearly and concisely and elaborate on them as needed."

A Little Secret About Communication

Few of us can take in, and remember, a list of facts and figures that is communicated to us. By our very nature we are forced to *interpret* what that list means.

The implications of this are enormous. If you present yourself based on your résumé, you give the interviewer the power to interpret the facts of your life. And just by ceding that right to them, you have put yourself in a weak position. You are in danger of becoming just another number in the system: another applicant like so many other applicants. You have given them an excuse to exclude you instead of a reason to include you.

However, when *you* interpret the facts, by framing them in a powerful infomercial, you're no longer in a weak position. You're not taking the risk the interviewer will come up with the wrong interpretation. You have handed the interpretation to them. Taking charge of what they see in itself signals that you are a strong prospect.

Your infomercial—your well-scripted story about *you*— can become second nature to you. It can become a mindset that gives you the power to get where you want to be by design, not default. Presenting yourself from this kind of strength is a lot more powerful than presenting yourself as the person whose name is on your résumé.

COUNTERING BAD INFOMERCIALS

You also need a Personal Infomercial to banish the one that's already out there, in many versions, none of which represents you accurately. It's your responsibility to make sure the world has a true and accurate infomercial about you. One that works hard for you instead of against you.

Good infomercials are not wishy-washy. They're not ambiguous. There's no fluff in them. No bafflegab. They never miss the point. They never veer from a clear and compelling description of your features, benefits, and value.

A Story About You

Your Personal Infomercial is your story. A story that is rich in value, insights, and information. It becomes so ingrained in your mind that you can deliver it naturally and spontaneously, anytime, anywhere. You can adapt its length to fit the circumstances, from an "elevator speech" to a job interview to an in-depth discussion about your goals and aspirations.

Although it is scripted, your infomercial never sounds scripted. Initially you write it out (numerous times), but when you deliver it you don't recite it verbatim. Rather, you deliver the most salient points based on the circumstances you're in. Your infomercial becomes a framework for you to draw on whenever you need it. You refine and adapt it on an ongoing basis.

Think of your infomercial as a rich renewable resource. Mine is embedded in my psyche. It gives me great confidence, in all situations.

I have helped hundreds of people create their infomercial. Each one used it as the foundation for finding the right fit for them. Many of them came back from interviews with compliments from the interviewer on the points they made and the excellent questions they asked.

A Screening Mechanism

Your infomercial can also act as a screening mechanism—for you. Delivering it will sometimes reveal to you that the position or firm is not right for you. Why? Because your infomercial clearly states what you want and need. It is a template that measures your fit. It helps you determine whether an organization or a person is a good match. It can save you, and others, a lot of time. If the fit isn't there, you know it's time to move on.

As you present yourself, you're are asking yourself the question, "Is this the right place for me?"

Wait a minute ... isn't the interviewer supposed to be asking if you're the right person for their *place? Not in your interviews.*

Another feature of your infomercial is how it causes you to exude confidence and control. As just mentioned, your infomercial helps you measure the company for fit. It turns the interview from one you're undergoing, to one you're giving. Big difference.

Make sure you don't include any false advertising in your infomercial. Make it straightforward and candid. It should include what you're *not* good at. It should include what is *not* a good fit for you. Finding your fit requires you to be open because fit is based on good relationships and good relationships are based on trust. Of course, the degree of candor depends on the person and the company you're talking to and the topic being discussed.

Before we get down to how you can begin to write and shape your Personal Infomercial, consider a few examples.

Dan's Personal Infomercial

Dan, introduced to you earlier in this chapter, was good at a lot of things, but by completing his Personal Balance Sheet he identified what he loved to do most. It was selling. Was he good at it? He had been at the top of several sales teams in major investment firms. And he had also built and managed a number of units within such businesses.

Dan's résumé was extensive, which is why it was initially difficult for him to whittle his infomercial down. In the end, he built it on several well-defined blocks of thought.

My passion is selling and building businesses. I am a deal

maker and a highly successful salesman. I am a roll-up-your-sleeves entrepreneur with excellent leadership skills.

I have built several units in major investment firms. I led one of them to over $220 million in sales.

I'm looking for an opportunity, not a "job." It can be with a start-up or an existing organization that needs to reach the next level of success.

What I am *not* interested in is being an operational-level person in a "second best" organization. I want to work with a growth company where my compensation is based on clear responsibilities and my performance.

Dan's delivery varies according to changing circumstances, but his core message always remains the same.

LEE'S PERSONAL INFOMERCIAL

Lee was an exceedingly bright Derivatives player. She had made a lot of money for the companies she had worked for. She had been given a lot of freedom to build businesses, hire people, and spend. Her bosses gave her plenty of air support and she had minimal bureaucracy to worry about.

As a result of changes in her business, however, Lee ended up looking for a new opportunity. She accepted an offer because she thought it was a good job in a good company. Unfortunately, the company was highly structured, requiring fifteen people's rubber stamp just to hire a receptionist. It was absolutely the wrong place for her.

Lee and I worked through the Personal Balance Sheet process and she created her infomercial. She was able to quote one of the senior people she had worked with as saying, "Give Lee six thousand square feet of space, a hundred people, and some capital and leave her alone. She'll make a lot of money for you." However, it turned out that no company was willing to put the reins in her hands the way she needed. Lee began to see that, in a sense, her TRE was herself. She decided to start her own company. She has never enjoyed her work more.

MY PERSONAL INFOMERCIAL

Once I was able to articulate my value, as a result of my Personal Balance Sheet exercises, I scripted my Personal Infomercial. I was relentless about it. I went over and over different versions of it until I had what I thought was right. Then I tested it on friends and colleagues and revised it again. Today I put forward a consistent infomercial, one that reflects the real me and gets across what I want to say.

People often say to me after I introduce myself, "Oh, you're in the head hunting business."

"No," I always say, "I'm a trusted advisor to my clients, helping them in recruiting, consulting on business matters, and coaching."

That happened to me just the other day on the golf course. A man in our foursome asked me what I did for a living.

"I'm a trusted advisor to my clients …," I said, giving him my infomercial.

"Really?" he said. "My wife works for ABC Company. She wants to switch careers. Do you think you could help her?"

If I had said, "I'm a head hunter," I would have become just another individual in another industry, prompting questions about where I had worked before, and so on.

Infomercials can do a lot of your work for you. I regularly hear mine played back to me. When people are referred to me and tell me why they want to talk to me, they use phrases from my infomercial. They say things like:

- Jim is a trusted advisor, a strategic extension of our business
- He provides great insight
- Jim has a superb understanding of people, organizations, and cultures. He is great at finding people who fit
- He helps you look around the corners, to see things you might otherwise miss

- It works best when you integrate him into your management team
- He is a valuable coach and mentor
- You will think differently and more clearly after talking with Jim

I couldn't have said it better myself.

Your Personal Infomercial

First, review the content of your Personal Balance Sheet exercises. Your findings will help you create your message. Look at the notes you've jotted down concerning:

(1) What you're good at, and evidence that supports what you say (three or four things, summarized)
(2) The type of people you therefore do and don't work best with (compatibility)
(3) The type of organizational culture you want (how you resolve conflicts)

Second, get the list of the companies you want to reach from your TRE.

And third, script your infomercial. Use these guidelines:

(1) Create a strong opening sentence that captures the main thing you're good at. It should create attention and interest.

- Dan: "My passion is selling and opening new client accounts"
- Lee: "I can make companies a lot of money when I'm given bandwidth and resources"
- Jim: "I'm a trusted advisor to my clients"

(2) Support your lead sentence with supporting sentences: succinct, specific statements of what you are good at.

- Dan: "I've been the number-one salesperson in three of the companies I've worked for"
- Lee: "When factors are in my control I can build a team and contribute a lot of money to the bottom line"
- Jim: "I am a trusted advisor to my clients, helping them by recruiting people, consulting on business matters, and coaching"

(3) Next, provide supporting evidence to the opening statement (simple facts; don't give too many details yet).

- Dan: "I built several new units in major corporations. I led one of them to over $220 million in sales"
- Lee: "At several companies where I've worked I was given the responsibility of building my own team and was given wide scope to lead it. My team led the entire company in sales"
- Jim: "I have hired over nine hundred people and am great at finding the right talent and fit. I'm a trusted and valuable resource to many international companies"

(4) State what you want and what you're looking for (types of people, work environment). Describe your fit.

(5) State what you do not want in terms of people (i.e., incompatibility) and company culture (i.e., conflict resolution).

(6) Make it clear what's most important to you.

- Dan: "I want to work with a growth company where my compensation is based on clear responsibilities and on my performance"
- Lee: "I'm looking for an organization that will give me plenty of scope to make them wealthy"

• Jim: "I'm looking for companies that both need my services and want me"

WORKING ON YOUR INFOMERCIAL

You will have to write several drafts of your infomercial before you are satisfied with it. Once you have it in a form that's acceptable to you, try it out on a few people. Start with a friend but also practice it on people who have worked with you and know you in terms of your skills and performance in the workplace. After you get this external feedback, you will be able to prepare your go-live version.

At every stage, practice, practice, practice.

Dan told me something interesting about how this process went for him.

"After I scripted my infomercial, I had to review it and repeat it to myself many times. That's the only way I could get it into my psyche."

It's the psyche that really matters. An infomercial that comes out of your psyche is more natural than one you're calling forth from your memory. You have to eat, sleep, and breathe your infomercial.

At first Dan found himself falling into the trap of being interviewed, versus interviewing the companies himself. He reverted to his old ways and walked interviewers through his résumé. But eventually his Personal Infomercial did become second nature to him. Now he can deliver it on demand.

Your goal is to make your infomercial a natural part of every conversation you have when the subject is you.

Variations on a Theme

Unlike a movie or book, there is no ending to your story. You will continually up-date your Personal Infomercial. As mentioned, you will also create variations on your main theme for different situations (telephone calls, interviews, introductions, leaving a job, conferences, cocktail parties, etc.).

The most important thing is to have a core message that is so *clear and concise that anyone can remember it*—and restate it over and over.

Fit Factor Tips

- You are not simply handing in a résumé and hoping an interviewer will see something in it and offer you a job. Use your Personal Infomercial to inspire interviewers to see the real you—to see what a good fit you would be for their company

- Use your Personal Infomercial to define you—instead of letting the rest of the world do so. Your infomercial creates a clear and accurate perception of the real you
- It is a rich renewable resource that becomes part of your psyche, a mindset that gives you the power to get where you want to go by design, not default
- Initially, write it out like a script and then revise and revise it, until you can deliver it naturally and spontaneously. Once it's ingrained in your mind, try it on several people
- Practice, practice, practice

Video link: You've read the chapter. Now see Jim online so he can help you work through the exercises. Join him at: **www.beqajinternational.com/perfectemployer**

How to Use Your Infomercial for Lasting Success

THE TOUGHEST THING ABOUT SUCCESS IS THAT
YOU'VE GOT TO KEEP ON BEING A SUCCESS.

Irving Berlin

YOU HAVE FIGURED OUT YOUR BEST FIT AND KNOW how to sell yourself into it. But there's another important part of the process: sustainability.

Once you have hired the perfect employer, it's up to you to sustain your fit, moving up to new heights in your company, if that's what you wish to do, or moving on to new responsibilities and opportunities elsewhere.

This chapter deals with the issue of sustainability in two ways:

- First, by discussing how you can use your Personal Infomercial on the job to sustain what you have learned in this book

- Second, by looking at the other half of the equation—organizations, whether large or small, and

what they can do to increase fit throughout
their ranks

I include the latter because I am aware that some of you
who are reading this book are in a position to affect the
way your organization seeks, finds, and supports fit. You
may be able to help your organization sharpen its policies
and practices in recruiting and developing human capital. I
hope this book can help bridge the "fit gap" by also getting
companies to start thinking more seriously and creatively
about fit.

Personal Sustainability

Let's assume you have found your best fit. How do you maintain it? How do you increase it?

Sheila came to me after she had accepted a high-level job at
a multinational corporation. Her situation demonstrates how
a Personal Infomercial not only helps people get into the right
job but also helps them build on it once they're in.

Sheila had been hired to head up a new division within a
very large and complex corporation. She quickly found herself
between a rock and a hard place. Much was expected of her,
but she hadn't been given a concrete game plan. The company

wasn't sure how the new initiative fit the company, much less how she fit the initiative.

Sheila had to start from scratch with minimal staff and support systems. She had been given a daunting task, but she was a bright, capable woman with great qualifications. She knew she was up to it.

What she didn't know was that she would be working sixteen hours a day juggling way too many responsibilities and expectations. It wasn't so much the number of hours that bothered her. It was that she could never get ahead of the problems.

To top it all off, others around her viewed her as in over her head.

"Having too much to do is never going to change," I told her. "That's just the way work is these days. So you should concentrate on the other challenges: priorities, expectations, and other people's perceptions."

Sheila was quite capable of setting priorities. Her challenge was managing the expectations and perceptions coming at her from her three prime constituencies: her boss and the senior executives; her staff; and the other departments in her division of the company (plenty of people were watching from the sidelines).

"A Personal Infomercial will help you communicate priorities and manage expectations and perceptions," I told her.

"That's it?" she said. "My boss recommended I come see you for advice on how to deal with my work overload. And you're talking to me about infomercials?"

I told her that regardless of what she wanted to achieve, in the end she would have to get people to understand what she was doing and win them over to her point of view.

"Senior executives don't expect everything to be served to them all at once," I said. "Right now they want quick wins. It's more about the next six months than anything else."

I showed her how a Personal Infomercial would help her define her success zone. And how this, in turn, would help her define her priorities: achievable priorities that *she* set.

Sheila worked with me to define the expectations of each group (people above, people below, and people laterally). She developed several core messages that matched those expectations. Through her Personal Infomercial, she broadcast which priorities were core ones. She stressed that she would be concentrating on them.

The main points in her infomercial were:

- Here are the priorities (this helped her get buy-in)
- Here's what we're doing to handle them (this provided people with evidence and prompted affirmation)
- Here are our expectations in terms of time lines (this helped her get agreement)

Later, Sheila created an elevator version for people who were not directly involved but were always asking, "How's it going?" She wanted to leave them feeling confidant that she was on top of things. She did so by creating these three perceptions for them:

- She had things in hand
- Things were getting better
- She wasn't satisfied but things were moving in the right direction

Her short version went like this:

There are a lot of priorities, but the key ones (insert 1 or 2) are on track and will happen in the next (30-60-90) days. Of course, there's much more to do, but the team is on top of the key issues (mention 1 or 2). I'm not satisfied that we're there yet, but we're making good progress.

Sheila's infomercial worked—again and again. It helped her with people in all three of her constituencies. The newness of her job and its lack of definition corporately were causing jumbled messages and perceptions to swirl around the company. Her infomercial not only played an important part in sustaining and advancing her own success, it also helped the company to integrate her initiative.

Day-to-Day Sustainability

Here are some scenarios to show you how the Personal Balance Sheet process you have followed in this book and the creation of your Personal Infomercial will help you sustain your fit on a daily basis.

- You're in a meeting and realize that others have a fuzzy view of you or your value. Through your infomercial you can give them an accurate and unambiguous version of who you are
- You're on a team where people resolve conflicts in different ways. You now have a grasp of your preferred way of handling conflicts and can spot the styles of others. You're able to see the differences on your team more clearly and can move to reconcile them and build on them
- You're asked to head up a project. Because of your greater self-knowledge, you realize that this project is not suited to your wiring. It doesn't fit what you're good at. Now you can communicate clearly why you

shouldn't take it on—or how it could be changed to take advantage of your skills

- Day in and day out you are expected communicate with different people and groups (clients, boss, peers, subordinates). Now you can address each audience and situation succinctly and professionally
- New opportunities arise in your organization. Because you know how to assess Target Rich Environments, you can decide which, if any, are worth pursuing

ORGANIZATIONAL SUSTAINABILITY

Let's shift our focus now to the responsibility of organizations to find people who fit.

A couple of years ago I met with a senior executive who had recently taken up a new position. Stephen was the head of a business unit in a large company.

He was concerned about major changes he needed to make in his unit. It wasn't contributing to the company's bottom line; this had come to light during a recent downturn in the markets.

I asked for more details and he filled me in on how he was planning to get his employees behind him to support and execute a major change in strategy.

"How's the depth of talent in your organization?" I asked. "Do you have the people you need to successfully execute your strategy?"

We went through his company's organizational structure. I asked more questions about the people in each position. By the time we were finished, Stephen let out a sigh.

"Wow. I've got a bigger mess than I thought," he said. "I've been looking at the business and the people but I've never looked closely at what is needed in each job to succeed. Obviously I'm going to have to review many positions and change some people if I expect to achieve real change."

Stephen's problem is all too common in organizations today. For numerous reasons, most of them do not connect *what success looks from the point of view of the CEO and board,* on the one hand, to *what success looks like at every level, in every job, of the organization,* on the other. They do not thoroughly assess what each job needs to do to succeed and whether the person in the job can deliver.

If this isn't done at every level and for every position, something very damaging happens: The level of success defaults to the weakest fit in the structure.

Stephen had been ignoring fit. He had not defined success, position by position. He had not determined whether the person in each position fit his unit's requirements for success.

Some companies get it right. General Electric under Jack Welch's leadership, for example. Also Isadore Sharp's Four Seasons Hotels and Resorts, where employee retention—an average of fifteen years for employees and twenty-two years for management—tells the tale.

Another example is a company in banking and finance I'm familiar with: Macquarie Group. With over thirteen thousand employees worldwide, Macquarie for years has developed and strengthened a great company culture. They attract great people. Like Four Seasons, it has a high retention rate.

But the majority of organizations have much work to do.

Most are filled with people who are capable and plenty talented but who are in the wrong jobs within the organization. Sustained success is not possible for a company with too many wrong fits.

It's a funny thing. Many companies do well despite this glaring lack of fit up and down their ranks. But they could do so much better if they had the right fits. Putting people in the right positions is an ongoing process in business. Companies aren't ever going to reach perfection, but it's important for them to try.

Fear is what's behind organizations' failure to focus on fit: fear of too much change, too much disruption, and too much expense. Organizations who bend to this fear avoid short-term pain—and as a result fail to realize any long-term gains.

"I can't believe they keep that guy here," someone says of an unproductive and disruptive person at work.

"Well, you know he's close to Don," someone else says.

"I can't believe they gave her a promotion," someone says.

"Well, they didn't have anyone else at the top who could slide in there."

This happens over and over in company after company in country after country. If leaders in these companies actually sat down and said, "Okay, do we have the right people on the team," they'd say no but chances are they'd be too lazy to go out and make things work.

"I know Steve and he's been around a long time," one of these leaders might say. "If I go out and take the time to find someone who fits and bring them up to speed with where we are in our plan ... And who knows what we're going to get?"

I just can't abide by this passive, fatalistic attitude, which is endemic to business today. When I worked in banking, I knew that just whipping a team harder and harder wouldn't do it if the people were the wrong fit. You can't force people to become something they're not, just like I can't say to a shy person, "I want you to spend five thousand a month entertaining clients and taking them to sports events, and golf games, and ..." It doesn't matter what I say, the person's not going to be able to do it, at least not on a sustained basis.

Companies need to understand that getting the right fit—the right people in the right positions in the right parts of the company—is good for everyone.

WHO IS NEEDED?

The first question for management relates to the job, *not the person*. Before you ask questions about any particular person in any particular job—or a new person being recruited—you have to decide what success looks like in the position, given the goals of the CEO, board, and senior leadership.

I'm not talking about a standard job description here; I'm talking about a description of success. It's not, primarily, about what a person will do ("lead," "head up," "be responsible for") but what the outcomes must be ("one million in sales," "ten percent growth," "ten percent increase in throughput").

I always ask, "What are the skills and personality type of the person that is needed to generate the outcomes in this particular job?" This is part of a broader examination of growth strategy and human capital and how they mesh in a corporation.

Let's focus briefly on the importance of finding the right individuals to fit a given position.

Profiling

After management has defined what success looks like in different positions, it should examine the profiles of the people in those positions, evaluating them on the basis of the skills, characteristics, and experience required by the positions.

These profiles must be done independently of the people who currently fill them. Knowledge of and feelings for an incumbent will create an inherent bias. Jobs too often get defined according to the incumbent's skills and personality rather than as a result of objective analysis.

Most companies accept these misconstrued descriptions. They move forward (or backward) by working with, and around, the problems that are created when square pegs are forced into round holes. The result? Dysfunction and under-performance.

Who Is Ideal?

Step back and ask the next critical question: "What does the ideal person look like in this job? What would they need to be good at? What skills would they have? What specific traits would they have? What type of people would they need to work with?"

You won't always find the ideal fit, but knowing what's needed for success will help you determine what the organization can do to supplement and support the person who is the best available fit.

More often than not, you'll see that people have been "moved up" to fill positions with little or no evaluation of their fit. They may have been good in their previous job. However, as we all know, success in one position doesn't automatically mean success in the next position. And yet this type of move is made over and over. Why? Because it's easier.

Once when I was running Fixed Income at the investment bank, the job of sales manager came open. One day one of the senior salesmen, Ted, sat down with me and said he wanted to apply for the job.

The underlying message was that he would quit if he didn't get it. This was bad timing for me because I needed every salesperson I had. Making things worse was the fact that Ted simply was not qualified for the manager's job.

I was faced with a dilemma. The more difficult one was to tell him straight out that there was no way I'd make him sales manager and risk his departure. The easier one was to make him sales manager and keep my numbers up. To do that, however, I would have to ignore the fact that, in the end, the business would suffer the consequences of a bad fit.

"Ted," I said, "before we talk about you being the sales manager, let me explain what success looks like in this job and what's required in it.

"First, a successful sales manager here is someone who has, and can build, senior account relationships. I require a guy who's going to be out three nights a week with clients, plus a weekend event every month. And there's lots of travel to Montreal and Vancouver. I also need the sales manager to lead the eight a.m. meeting and to be one of the last to leave because we have to set an example for the junior salespeople. Basically, that's the fit for this job."

I went on to talk about him.

"Ted, based on what I have seen, I have some questions about how you would fit in this job. Looking at your expense accounts, I have never seen anything related to evenings and weekends with clients. You just don't spend time or money building relationships and that's essential for the sales manager. I know you like to coach—a baseball team and a hockey team, right?—and you catch the five o'clock train home, every day. So there's a question of time availability and commitment.

"And, let's face it," I added, "you're not among the top three sales producers. And, as far as I know, you've never helped a junior on the job."

After we discussed the critical success factors in the sales manager's job, I said, "If you want the job, it's available. But first, go home and ask yourself if the job as I describe it is what you want. Not just the title, but the job. If it is, I'll pay you well, but you must be certain that you can do what is required."

Several days later Ted told me the job wasn't for him. Fortunately, he didn't quit.

But on that day when he initially confronted me with his expectation, I was prepared to say no and let him go if he didn't like it. Why? Because long term, putting him in the wrong position would have hurt the organization.

As a manager, you have to be prepared to put fit before almost anything else. Because if you don't, you're going to get yourself leveraged into a boatload of dysfunction, negativity, and underperformance.

Start with a clear description of success for the position and then create the ideal description of the person who can meet the requirements for success. That defines the best fit. And if it isn't Ted, don't promote him. Go find the right person.

I recommend this method to leaders and managers who are trying to achieve the best fit in the positions they manage. This process of describing expectations to an applicant often leads them to opt out.

Setting Expectations

Whenever I was responsible for building a business unit—whether within the bank or when the bank was taking over a business—I began by stating a clear vision of what success would look like. Then I set out a course of direction—a series of principles, rules, and regulations—for the work environment.

This approach is essential if you want to get the right outcomes. Why? Because outcomes are the result of people's behaviors, and those behaviors are the result of understanding expectations and the consequences of not meeting expectations.

Using figure 7.1, let's look at what happens when you take this approach.

There's always a group of early adopters ("A"): people who like clarity, principles, and a vision of success they can believe in.

Next, there's a percentage of people who wait and see and could go either way ("B1" and "B2"). It's up to the leader to show them why it's better for them to get on board. They need to be aware that they have to make a clear-cut decision to either get on board or off.

Some of them will resist the new way. It may sound harsh, but you have to get rid of these people. Most organizations aren't prepared to do this because this group usually represents long-standing, unproductive employees.

In my experience, a strong leader can get as many as three out of four of the B1s to join the early adopters. The B2s slip into the lowest, never-going-to-get-on-board group ("C"). They don't fit and they're not going to try to fit. The number of people in this group can vary. Regardless of their numbers, they pose a serious problem to the rest of the organization. Even a few people like this can drag everyone else down. They have to be weeded out.

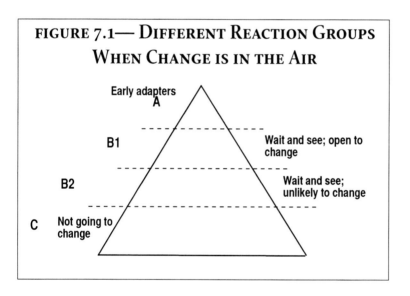

FIGURE 7.1— DIFFERENT REACTION GROUPS WHEN CHANGE IS IN THE AIR

If you don't deal with this reality, you can kiss building sustainable growth goodbye. It can't be achieved. The resisters and those who can't adapt will always be pulling the organization in the wrong direction. And eventually this will affect—infect—everyone.

The A and B1 groups know that they're onside and doing all the right things, but they watch the sideliners, who are getting the same pay and benefits while underperforming. The resentment the A and B1 groups feel can turn them into average performers. The C group, meanwhile, isn't doing the company any favors. It's obvious that they don't fit.

Companies are often reluctant to address this hidden cost because it is not easily measured ("what isn't measured doesn't get done"). It seems easier to them to work around "a few" bad fits than go through serious change.

When a company fails to address fit, it expends—and wastes—an inordinate amount of time, energy, and money in managing, reconciling, compensating, pacifying, and arbitrating the divide between the disparate groups. It's a huge cost burden.

No Shortage of Talent

I often ask CEOs if they're prepared to get rid of the people who don't fit and don't buy into the requirements for success. Interestingly, they often say they're afraid if they do they won't be able to find enough of the right people. That is unfounded. There is no lack of talent out there that would be a better fit.

The problem stems from not properly defining fit and from not knowing what to look for. And from not being committed to look for it—constantly.

Few companies mine *their* Target Rich Environment of employees. This is primarily because they have not fully defined that environment. Also, most companies do not search for talent on an ongoing basis. They tend to cite a lack of time and/or the extra cost of continually searching.

Successful sports franchises understand the critical importance of continuously scouting for the right talent and the right fit. This kind of scouting starts early and never ends. Most professional players are spotted in high school and scouted for years. Some become winners and some do not. But most of those who make it are a good fit. Sport focuses on talent because winning depends on talent.

The same is true of business in general. The right or wrong talent, at every position, is what separates the champions from the also-rans.

Talent Scouts

Every business must develop a systematic and continuous process of defining the talent it requires and scouting for it. It cannot be a periodic, when-the-need-arises activity. The scouting process of a business must start early and never end, because most businesses are constantly changing as they adapt to markets and redefine needs. If you don't know who the good guys and bad guys are or where they are—whether in your company or in the market—you're not going to improve. Growth comes from continual improvement and improvement comes from continuously upgrading your talent—talent that fits.

The people responsible for the long-term development of the corporation's human capital must have an integrated process that links the organization's strategy to every position and every person in each position. In sports, the scouts are hardly ever at their desk. They're out in the field talking, meeting, searching. The only way to find the best is to fully understand the fits you need in your business, to be fully versed in what's available in the marketplace, and to constantly pursue the best talent—the best fits.

Great organizations reach greatness by design, not default. They attract top talent because the best people want to work in places where meritocracy and fit are first principles.

Of course, it's more difficult to deal with the issue of fit by design rather than default. Handling it by design means more work and—in the beginning—more turnover. It means more time and higher short-term costs. But I ask: What more important investment could there be than the fit of your human capital?

Fit Factor Tips

- Use your Personal Infomercial and what you learned through the Personal Balance Sheet process to continually shape and sustain your fit
- Corporations are the other half of the fit equation and it's essential that they, too, understand the critical nature of fit
- In a corporation, determining fit begins with defining what success looks like in any position and then looking for the individual who best fits that definition
- There is no dearth of talent; organizations must search continuously for the right talent and the right fit for that talent
- It's not easy for an organization to make the necessary changes to build its investment in human capital on the basis of the Fit Factor, but those who do it are always the best at what they do

Video link: You've read the chapter. Now see Jim online so he can help you work through the content of this chapter. Join him at:

www.beqajinternational.com/perfectemployer

CONCLUSION

I STARTED THIS BOOK BY NOTING A GREAT IRONY IN THE world of work today: that while organizations say their number-one challenge is finding people who fit, most people, whether they are already employed or are looking for an employer, say finding the right fit is *their* biggest challenge.

Now that you've read this book, you can help bridge this gap—whether you are heading out with your Personal Infomercial to find a great job or are part of an organization that is welcoming the best talent and fit into its ranks.

AFTERWORD

By Tom Milroy

I first knew Jim Beqaj as a colleague in the capital markets business. I followed his progress with great interest when he left the business and reinvented himself, to the point of actually creating his own company.

Perhaps "reinvented himself" is not the right way to put it in Jim's case. Jim did not come up with a totally new life for himself in business. Rather, he is now doing, full-time and on his own, what he enjoyed most and did best as just one of his many responsibilities in his previous work. He is helping to bring individuals and organizations together in ways that fit the culture and values of both.

I know Jim's career experiences and life experiences coalesced to make him look more deeply both into himself and others, on the one hand, and into businesses and business organizations, on the other, as he considered what he was going to pursue going forward. It was gratifying for me to see how this deeper understanding fueled his new efforts.

I have experienced first-hand in our organization how well Jim grasps the culture and values of the organization he is helping in order to find people who truly fit. And in addition to our formal relationship, I have found it productive to talk to Jim about how I was looking at management and human resources issues with respect to my own business responsibilities.

With the publication of this book, Jim is taking his insights about fit to a new and broader audience. This definitely bodes well for the workforce of tomorrow.

Tom Milroy is Chief Executive Officer,
BMO Capital Markets.

ABOUT JIM BEQAJ

BEQAJ INTERNATIONAL INC.

Trusted Advice. Human Solutions.

Jim Beqaj began his career in 1977 in the investment banking firm Wood Gundy. He rose quickly through the ranks and in 1992, at the age of thirty-seven, became President of that firm, which was wholly owned by CIBC. Following that he worked as Vice Chairman of Bank of Montreal and then co-founded an innovative Internet-based IPO company, BAYSTREETDIRECT.COM. In 2002 he poured his always unorthodox methods of building businesses, attracting talent, and developing leaders into the founding of his new firm, Beqaj International Inc., through which he acts as a trusted advisor for financial institutions and individuals worldwide, providing them with recruiting, consulting, and coaching services.

THE BEQAJ PHILOSOPHY

Indecision is a killer.

Be confident in your choices.

Wrong decisions will produce better results than no
decision at all.

Besides, mistakes are essential to progress.

The willingness to learn from them is the backbone of progress.

The objective is to succeed, not count your mistakes.

www.beqajinternational.com

CPSIA information can be obtained at www.ICGtesting.com
Printed in the USA
LVOW010406181011

250889LV00003B/7/P